W9-CDG-971

Easter

Buddy BOOKS
Holidays

ABDO
Publishing Company

A Buddy Book
by
Julie Murray

VISIT US AT
www.abdopublishing.com

Published by ABDO Publishing Company, 8000 West 78th Street, Edina, Minnesota 55439.

Copyright © 2012 by Abdo Consulting Group, Inc. International copyrights reserved in all countries. No part of this book may be reproduced in any form without written permission from the publisher. Buddy Books™ is a trademark and logo of ABDO Publishing Company.

Printed in the United States of America, North Mankato, Minnesota.
052011
092011

♻ PRINTED ON RECYCLED PAPER

Coordinating Series Editor: Rochelle Baltzer
Editor: Sarah Tieck
Contributing Editors: Megan M. Gunderson, BreAnn Rumsch, Marcia Zappa
Graphic Design: Denise Esner
Cover Photograph: *Shutterstock*: Murat Subatli.
Interior Photographs/Illustrations: *AP Photo*: Charles Dharapak (p. 11), Randy Dockendorf/
     Daily Press & Dakotan (p. 21), Jose Luis Magana (pp. 9, 19), L'Osservatore Romano
     (p. 22), Richard Thomas/Detroit News (p. 21); *iStockphoto*: ©iStockphoto.com/
     abalcazar (p. 9), ©iStockphoto.com/dndavis (p. 12), ©iStockphoto.com/hartcreations
     (p. 5), ©iStockphoto.com/itsjustluck (p. 15), ©iStockphoto.com/JLBarranco (p. 11),
     ©iStockphoto.com/2ndLookGraphics (p. 13); *Shutterstock*: KIS (p. 16), Nick Lawson
     (p. 17), Robyn Mackenzie (p. 18), Teri and Jack Soares (p. 7).

Library of Congress Cataloging-in-Publication Data

Murray, Julie, 1969-
  Easter / Julie Murray.
     p. cm. -- (Holidays)
  ISBN 978-1-61783-038-9
  1. Easter--Juvenile literature. I. Title.
  GT4935.M87 2012
  394.2667--dc22
                         2011002285

Table of Contents

What Is Easter?

Easter is an important Christian holiday. On this day, many Christians spend time praying or attending church. Family and friends share food and fun.

Easter is on a different date each year. But, it is usually on a Sunday in March or April. So for many people, Easter means the arrival of spring.

On Easter, children often receive baskets filled with gifts and treats.

The Easter Story

For around 2,000 years, Christians have observed Easter. It is a celebration of Jesus Christ's resurrection.

The Bible includes many stories and teachings about Jesus. Jesus was a Christian leader. His followers believed he was the Son of God.

But, other people strongly disagreed with Jesus's teachings. They sentenced him to die on a cross.

Crosses are an important Christian symbol. They are seen on churches and in Christian art.

After Jesus died, he was put in a tomb. That Sunday, he rose from the dead. His followers were amazed! This became known as Easter Sunday.

The 40 days before Easter is a time called Lent. Christians pray and prepare for Easter during Lent. Some people do not eat certain foods.

The week before Easter is called Holy Week. During Holy Week, many Christians attend church and observe traditions.

For many Christians, Lent begins on Ash Wednesday. Some people attend church on this day. Church leaders mark a cross with ash on their foreheads.

Palm Sunday is one week before Easter. On this day, many churches hand out palm branches or crosses. This is because people honored Jesus with palm branches before he died.

Signs of Life

Many holidays have special symbols. Easter symbols often stand for hope and new life. They remind Christians of Jesus's resurrection.

Easter eggs are one symbol of new life. Many people decorate eggs. And, Easter egg hunts and egg rolls are common traditions.

The White House Easter Egg Roll takes place every year in Washington, D.C.

Some families dye Easter eggs. This makes the eggs look special. And, it brings spring colors into their homes.

An Easter lily is a flower. It is a **symbol** of pure new life. Around Easter, these flowers decorate churches.

Lilies are mentioned in several parts of the Bible. Easter lilies are known for their white petals and strong smell.

In the United States, Easter lilies are very popular! People often buy them to honor or remember loved ones.

The Easter Bunny

Easter takes place during spring. Spring is a time of new life for many plants and animals. Rabbits are a symbol of new life.

Around the 1700s, Germans began sharing stories of an egg-laying bunny. Over time, the story became a part of the Easter celebration.

The word *Easter* may have come from Eostre, a goddess of spring and new life. One symbol of Eostre is a hare, which looks like a rabbit (*above*).

Today on Easter, children often receive baskets from the Easter Bunny. They are filled with candy, decorated eggs, and other small gifts.

Fabergé eggs are some of the most famous Easter eggs. They are decorated with jewels and often filled with treasures!

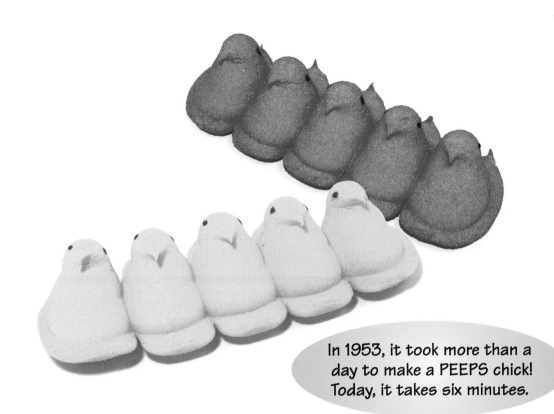

In 1953, it took more than a day to make a PEEPS chick! Today, it takes six minutes.

Candy is a big part of Easter. People buy almost as much candy for Easter as they do for Halloween! Famous Easter candies are jelly beans, chocolate bunnies, and PEEPS Brand Marshmallow Candies.

Food and Fun

On Easter, many people make a special meal. **Traditional** foods include ham, lamb, hot cross buns, and pretzels.

Hot cross buns have a frosting cross on them. Some Christians used to give these to the poor.

Since around 1840, a famous Passion play has taken place yearly in Iztapalapa, Mexico. The entire town is the stage and locals are the actors!

Some people take part in Easter parades or Passion plays. A Passion play retells the Easter story.

Easter Today

Easter remains an important Christian holiday around the world. On this day, Christians take time to think about Jesus's resurrection.

For Christians, Easter means the promise of new life after death. Easter eggs and the Easter Bunny help celebrate this promise!

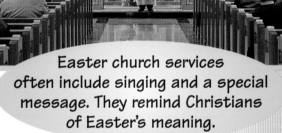

Easter church services often include singing and a special message. They remind Christians of Easter's meaning.

Easter around the World

- Every year in Italy, the pope gives an Easter message. The pope is a **Christian** leader.

- Instead of the Easter Bunny, flying bells bring treats to children in France.

Pope Benedict XVI

- In Greece, Russia, eastern Europe, and western Asia many people are Eastern Orthodox Christians. They often honor Easter on a different Sunday.

Important Words

celebrate to observe a holiday with special events. These events are known as celebrations.

Christian (KRIHS-chuhn) a person who practices Christianity, which is a religion that follows the teachings of Jesus Christ.

resurrection (reh-zuh-REHK-shuhn) the act of rising from the dead or returning to life.

symbol (SIHM-buhl) an object or mark that stands for an idea.

tomb (TOOM) a special building or structure that houses the dead.

tradition (truh-DIH-shuhn) a belief, a custom, or a story handed down from older people to younger people.

Web Sites

To learn more about Easter,
visit ABDO Publishing Company online. Web sites about Easter are featured on our Book Links page. These links are routinely monitored and updated to provide the most current information available.

www.abdopublishing.com

Index